INTERACTIVE WORKBOOK

THE POWER OF JESUS' NAMES

TONY EVANS

HARVEST HOUSE PUBLISHERS
EUGENE, OREGON

Cover design by Bryce Williamson

Cover photo © Pearl / Lightstock

The Power of Jesus' Names Interactive Workbook
Copyright © 2019 by Tony Evans
Published by Harvest House Publishers
Eugene, Oregon 97408
www.harvesthousepublishers.com

ISBN 978-0-7369-7608-4 (pbk.)

Printed in the United States of America

20 21 22 23 24 25 26 27 / VP-SK / 10 9 8

CONTENTS

Acknowledgments

I want to thank my friends at Harvest House Publishers for their long-standing partnership in bringing my thoughts, study, and words to print. I particularly want to thank Bob Hawkins for his friendship over the years, as well as his pursuit of excellence in leading his company. I also want to publicly thank Terry Glaspey, Betty Fletcher, and Amber Holcomb for their help in the editorial process.

Working with the team at Right Now Media is always a pleasure, and they bring great professionalism and talent to what they do, as well as a love for our Lord. Thank you, Phil Warner, for leading your group so well, and many thanks to the entire team who both filmed and edited this study in Israel. In addition, my appreciation goes out to Heather Hair for her skills and insights in collaboration on this Bible study content and assistance with the video production.

MAKING THE MOST OF THIS INTERACTIVE WORKBOOK

This interactive workbook is a tool to help your group combine the video and Bible study into a dynamic growth experience. If you are the leader or facilitator of your group, take some time in advance to consider the questions in the Video Group Discussion and Group Bible Exploration portions of this guide and prepare your own personal examples to encourage discussion. To get the most out of this study, each group member should have their own copy of this workbook. This will allow them to take notes during the group time and to dig deeper on their own throughout the week.

Every group session includes a video portion, so consider the logistics in advance. Will everyone be able to see the screen clearly? Make sure to set the audio at a comfortable level before the session. You don't want your group to miss anything.

With that in mind, let's preview the guide. Each lesson has six sections:

Video Teaching Notes

Several key points and quotes from the video are provided in this section, but there's also room to write your own notes.

Video Group Discussion

People in your group are likely to forget the content unless they review it right away. Many of the discussion questions have to do with remembering what they just viewed. But other questions try to connect the video to their emotions or experience. *How did you feel when he said that? Is that true in your life? Do you have the same issue?*

Group Bible Exploration

This is a Bible study, so each session is grounded in Scripture. Your group members may have different levels of faith. This is a time to open up the Bible and grow as a group or help others find their faith.

In Closing

The goal for every Bible study is to apply what you've learned. This section will highlight the main point of the lesson and challenge your group to spend some time diving deeper into the week's theme.

On Your Own Between Sessions

This section includes additional study individuals can do to keep the content they just learned fresh in their minds throughout the week and to put it into practice.

Recommended Reading

Your group time in this video Bible study will be enhanced if everyone takes the time to read the recommended chapters in *The Power of Jesus' Names* by Tony Evans. Dr. Evans' video teaching follows the book, but the book includes considerably more information and illustrations. If you are the leader, encourage your group to prepare ahead.

SESSION 1

IMMANUEL

The name Immanuel originated within a context of pain, despair, loss, doubt, fear, and chaos. Immanuel came to a world in crisis. It is not merely a name to remember during Christmas as we sing carols and drink hot chocolate. No, Immanuel is a name of comfort when times are at their worst.

One of the first things you need to understand about Jesus is that no matter what you have gone through or are currently going through, He is with you. No matter how difficult the challenges you face, God is with you. No matter how many enemies attack you—whether internally or externally—God is with you. Whatever you are facing, struggling with, enduring, or exhausted from, God is with you. The birth of Jesus Christ is not only the introduction of our Savior into this world; it is also the introduction of God's promise of victory and His presence in the midst of a painful reality we all know far too well.

Friend, God is with you. Jesus came that we may know God more fully and experience His power more completely as He deals with our sins and our circumstances.

This is one of the primary things I want you to understand as we begin our look at Jesus' names. No matter what you have gone through, you are not alone. No matter what difficulties have threatened to drown you, you can overcome. No matter what challenges you are facing—however big or small—God's victory is in your grasp because God's presence is with you. You are not facing anything on your own.

When Matthew introduced the name Immanuel by referring back to Isaiah, he reminded his readers, who were suffering under Roman oppression, of the prophecy's context. He ensured them of the presence of God in a decaying and challenging season. He emphasized that this entry of Immanuel into our world was a reminder that God is with each of us—even, and especially, when things are not in our favor. Jesus gives us God in the flesh. Colossians 1:15 puts it this way: "He is the image of the invisible God, the firstborn of all creation." He is "the exact representation" of God (Hebrews 1:3).

When we talk about Jesus—Immanuel—we are talking about God Himself. We are not just talking about a man who lived and died on earth. This is God in the flesh.

The Power of Jesus' Names, pages 20-22

Video Teaching Notes

As you watch the video, use the spaces below to take notes. Some key points and quotes are provided here as reminders.

Teaching: Immanuel

Jesus is the exact representation of God. In Him, all the fullness of deity dwells (Colossians 2:9). If you want to see or experience God, just look to Jesus.

Isaiah points out some very practical effects of having Jesus with us in the form of Immanuel. He calls Him the Wonderful Counselor, Mighty God, Eternal Father, and the Prince of Peace (Isaiah 9:6). Take a moment to describe briefly each of these attributes of Immanuel.

The power and purpose of the incarnation is that God becomes experientially real to you through the person of Jesus—Immanuel.

This video segment was filmed at the location in Bethlehem where it is believed Jesus was born. As you can see in the video, the area is now built up with churches and elaborate decorations. Contrast the present state of this location with how things were when Jesus was born. Why do you think God would have Immanuel ("God with us") be born in an obscure location lacking comfort and notoriety?

Quotables

- Jesus is the eternal emulsifier. He is fully God. He is fully man. And by faith in Him, God and man are brought together.

- If you belong to Jesus Christ, you're walking around with God in the midst of your life.

- We call this the incarnation: God becoming a man, deity being poured into humanity. The theological term for this is the *hypostatic union*, where there are two natures in one person, unmixed forever.

Video Group Discussion

1. In the video, Dr. Evans teaches on the scriptural truth that Jesus is fully God and fully man. Describe the effects of combining these two natures. How does it impact Jesus' relationship with you on a daily basis?

2. The teaching on Immanuel was filmed in Bethlehem. Visitors come from all around the world and wait in line for hours in order to enter the area where it is believed that Jesus was born. Once they enter, they are given less than a minute to see it and then move on to make room for more people. In some ways, this is symbolic of the wise men traveling far at great personal cost to worship the young King. Why is it important to worship Jesus?

    a. Romans 12:1 says, "I urge you, brethren, by the mercies of God, to present your bodies a living and holy sacrifice, acceptable to God, which is your spiritual service of worship." How is this another way of worshiping Jesus?

    b. What are some specific things you can do to apply the worship described in Romans 12:1 to your everyday life?

c. Standing in line for hours, awaiting the opportunity to pass by a monument symbolizing where the birth of Jesus occurred, takes great commitment and discipline. In what ways can you apply greater commitment and personal discipline to how you worship Jesus in your daily life?

3. Dr. Evans uses the example of mayonnaise to illustrate how Jesus joins God and humanity. What keeps God and humanity separate to begin with?

a. How does the joining of God and humanity through Jesus give you greater access to spiritual power?

b. Can you come up with another illustration to demonstrate how Immanuel joins God and humanity? Get creative. You might want to work on this together as a group.

4. Dr. Evans says that Jesus is God's selfie. With that picture in mind, read each of the following passages and write them in your own words. Then take some time to share how each verse applies to your life.

a. "Those whom He foreknew, He also predestined to become conformed to the image of His Son, so that He would be the firstborn among many brethren" (Romans 8:29).

b. "Be imitators of me, just as I also am of Christ" (1 Corinthians 11:1).

c. "A pupil is not above his teacher; but everyone, after he has been fully trained, will be like his teacher" (Luke 6:40).

5. Jesus is God's selfie, and in a way, we are called to be Jesus' selfie—to reflect His character, will, and attributes in our daily lives. Share a specific way you can do that this week.

Group Bible Exploration

1. Read the following shaded verses together. Describe the similarities between the name of God listed before each verse and what the passage says about Jesus.

   a. Elohim (Creator)

   > By Him all things were created, both in the heavens and on earth, visible and invisible, whether thrones or dominions or rulers or authorities—all things have been created through Him and for Him (Colossians 1:16).

   b. Jehovah (I Am)

   > Jesus said to them, "Truly, truly, I say to you, before Abraham was born, I am" (John 8:58).

c. Jehovah Nissi (Banner of Victory)

These things I have spoken to you, so that in Me you may have peace. In the world you have tribulation, but take courage; I have overcome the world (John 16:33).

d. Jehovah Rohi (Shepherd)

I am the good shepherd; the good shepherd lays down His life for the sheep (John 10:11).

e. El Elyon (High and Mighty)

Far above all rule and authority and power and dominion, and every name that is named, not only in this age but also in the one to come (Ephesians 1:21).

2. Read the following passage together and then describe the difference between the first order and the second order. Why was it necessary that God become a sinless man in order to satisfy the demands of the first order?

> When He comes into the world, He says, "Sacrifice and offering You have not desired, but a body You have prepared for Me; in whole burnt offerings and sacrifices for sin You have taken no pleasure. Then I said, 'Behold, I have come (in the scroll of the book it is written of Me) to do Your will, O God.'" After saying above, "Sacrifices and offerings and whole burnt offerings and sacrifices for sin You have not desired, nor have You taken pleasure in them" (which are offered according to the Law), then He said, "Behold, I have come to do Your will." He takes away the first in order to establish the second (Hebrews 10:5-9).

3. Read the following verses together. What is the difference between being "given" and being "sent"? Why do you think this distinction is made?

> A child will be born to us, a son will be given to us (Isaiah 9:6).

> When the time came to completion, God sent His Son, born of a woman, born under the law (Galatians 4:4 HCSB).

Notice that one word: *given*. The Son was given by God. As the Son of God, Jesus already existed, but He came to earth through human birth. That's why it could be said of Him that He created the universe. Too many people want to keep Jesus in the manger because they don't want to deal with His deity. As long as they can keep Him asleep in the stable, they don't have to reckon with the reality that He's God on a throne. But He was already God. Thus, the Son had to be "given."

The Power of Jesus' Names, pages 16-17

4. How does understanding that Jesus is both a man who had to be born but also God who was sent from heaven affect your view of Christmas?

In Closing

As you end the group study today, spend some time sharing prayer requests related to your relationship with Jesus and your understanding of His names. Be specific when addressing the areas you feel you need to grow in the most. Ask Jesus to open your hearts throughout this study in order that each of you may come to Him like never before. Also ask that He will guard and protect your priorities and time in order to enable each of you to finish this study in its entirety.

Before moving on to session 2, complete the On Your Own Between Sessions section below.

On Your Own Between Sessions

1. In the book *The Power of Jesus' Names*, Dr. Evans recounts the story of a wealthy man who chose to give his entire inheritance to whoever bid on the picture of his only son at his estate auction after his death. The person who valued the son enough to purchase the picture gained everything. In what ways do you devalue Jesus, God's Son, through your choices, purchases, or words?

In what ways can you value Jesus more? List something specific you can do this week.

2. Read John 1:18.

   a. In what ways has Jesus "explained" God?

b. List seven attributes of Jesus that give a reflection of God the Father we would not have known apart from Jesus revealing Him to us.

    1.

    2.

    3.

    4.

    5.

    6.

    7.

Jesus took everything there was to know about God and put it on a shelf we could reach. Jesus is the complete revelation of God. That's why you can't bypass Jesus and get to God. You can't skip Jesus and have God. You can't deny Jesus and know God. Jesus is the only begotten Son—the only one. Jesus is *God with us*. He is Immanuel.

The Power of Jesus' Names, page 19

3. How do people seek to "skip Jesus" in our culture today?

Pray and ask God to give you wisdom and insight into any areas of your life where you are not openly forthright about Jesus. Then ask Him to provide you with the boldness you need to proclaim Jesus in and through all you do.

Life Exercise: Getting Intimate with Jesus

1. *Identify* a time when you can focus on Jesus each day. In the book of John, this is called "abiding."

2. *Consider* several ways to nurture your relationship with Jesus during this time. For example, you could write in a journal any thoughts you have toward Him or thank Him for any of His attributes. Or you could look up Scripture about Jesus and meditate on it for a few minutes.

3. *Evaluate* how your relationship deepens as you spend consistent time with Immanuel throughout the week. Also evaluate whether or not it becomes easier to proclaim Jesus through your words and actions the more you abide in Him.

4. *Repeat.* After you've put this practice into play this week, seek to repeat it in the weeks to come. You can incorporate the various aspects of Jesus we'll be studying into your daily intimate time with Him.

Recommended Reading

In preparation for session 2, you may want to read chapter 6 of *The Power of Jesus' Names*. To review the material from session 1, read chapter 1.

SESSION 2

LORD AND KING

The entire Old Testament speaks in anticipation of this coming King who would one day rule on earth from the perspective of heaven. He would come through the Jews, sit on the throne of David, and oversee and rule the world from Israel. The prophets anticipated this King. God's covenant with Abraham anticipated this King. David's royal lineage anticipated this King. Zechariah 9:9 gives us insight into the thoughts of those who looked for King Jesus:

> Rejoice greatly, O daughter of Zion! Shout in triumph, O daughter of Jerusalem! Behold, your king is coming to you; He is just and endowed with salvation, humble, and mounted on a donkey, even on a colt, the foal of a donkey.

We shouldn't be surprised that when Jesus was ready to reveal His kingship, He told His disciples to get Him a donkey, since it had been prophesied that the divine King would ride on one. We shouldn't be shocked that the magi came to worship Him after His birth, claiming that He was born King of the Jews (Matthew 2:2). When John the Baptist announced the King's arrival, he phrased it in terms the nation of Israel could understand: "Repent, for the kingdom of heaven is at hand" (Matthew 3:2). And when Jesus began preaching, He stepped onto the stage of history and said the same thing. "From that time Jesus began to preach and say, 'Repent, for the kingdom of heaven is at hand' " (Matthew 4:17). Furthermore, as He sent His disciples to preach, He told them to proclaim the kingdom of God had arrived (Matthew 10:7).

The King had come. His name was Jesus.

[Yet] when we speak of Jesus, one of the names we aren't so quick to call Him by in today's culture—although it was hugely attributed to Him throughout all Scripture—is King. We recognize Him as Savior. We see that He is the living Lamb. We sing about Him as Immanuel. We tend to portray or visualize Jesus primarily in redemptive roles. And while these roles are key, I am afraid that in focusing so heavily on them, we miss out on much of Jesus' power in our daily lives. This power shows up in the names we get to know and align ourselves under, such as King, Lord, and Great High Priest.

Sure, redemption appeals to us in our autonomous, me-centric culture. We tend to be highly independent and self-serving, and many would even argue that our culture has given rise to an epidemic of narcissistic thinking. To acknowledge Jesus as King conjures up responses of obedience, dependence, honor, respect, and self-sacrifice. It goes against what our culture tells us is the way to live our lives.

Regardless, Jesus is King.

The Power of Jesus' Names, pages 47-48

Video Teaching Notes

As you watch the video, use the spaces below to take notes. Some key points and quotes are provided here as reminders.

Teaching 1: Lord

To affirm Jesus as Lord is to affirm Him as God. Many people recognize Jesus as God but do not want to submit to Him as Lord, so they do not get the benefits of His deity operating in their lives. Are you willing to call Jesus "Lord" like Thomas did when he saw Him after the resurrection? (See John 20:26-28.) Affirming Jesus as Lord opens the door for Him to intervene in your everyday life.

Teaching 2: King

A king rules over a realm, and within that realm live the citizens of that kingdom.

The kingdom agenda is the visible manifestation of the comprehensive rule of God over every area of life. As subjects to the King, we are to align our thoughts and actions under that comprehensive rule.

All of us have to ask ourselves, "Does Jesus Christ rule? Do His perspective and will call the final shots in my life?"

Quotables

- If you are a secret-agent Christian, you are denying Jesus' lordship. When you deny His lordship, you deny His intervention. And when you deny His intervention, you're not getting the benefits of His deity.

- The lordship of Jesus Christ has to do with His intervention in your life.

- It is unfortunate that many Christians today are satisfied with being religious on Sunday, while denying His lordship all week long. As a result, they don't find out what His will is. They simply ask Him to bless their will, and they lose the divine intervention.

Video Group Discussion

1. In the video, Dr. Evans tells us that to honor Jesus as Lord means that He must not merely be prominent; He must be preeminent. Describe the difference between the two and give an example of how this shows up in a person's spiritual walk.

2. The teaching on Jesus as Lord was filmed in Capernaum, a village on the northern side of the Sea of Galilee. During Jesus' lifetime, Capernaum had up to 1,500 residents, many of whom were farmers and fishermen. The area is one of the more frequently mentioned locations in the Bible, and Jesus spent a large part of His ministry time there. In Luke 4:31-35, He performed a miracle in Capernaum by driving out a demon from a man on the Sabbath. Read that passage and then reflect on the following questions.

   a. How did the demonic man refer to Jesus? What does this reveal to us about the evil realm?

b. Why were the people "amazed" by Jesus' teaching in the synagogue?

3. Dr. Evans uses the example of the authority he has in his home to illustrate God's authority within the world He created. What would happen if you had no rules or expectations for those who live in your home?

    a. Describe what would happen if "squatter's rights" meant anyone and everyone could enter and use your home.

    b. How should this affect the way we view our role in respecting God's rule in the world He has created?

4. Dr. Evans lists two ways we can react to the role of Jesus as King in our lives. What are these two options?

    a. Is "ignoring" Jesus as King a third option? Why or why not?

    b. What are some of the practical consequences a person can face when he or she does not honor or view Jesus as King over their life?

Group Bible Exploration

Read the shaded verses together and answer the questions that follow.

> He is the image of the invisible God, the firstborn of all creation. For by Him all things were created, both in the heavens and on earth, visible and invisible, whether thrones or dominions or rulers or authorities—all things have been created through Him and for Him. He is before all things, and in Him all things hold together. He is also head of the body, the church; and He is the beginning, the firstborn from the dead, so that He Himself will come to have first place in everything (Colossians 1:15-18).

1. With the resurrection and exaltation of Jesus Christ, He has been made head over all rulers and authorities. He is in charge. What is the difference between power and authority?

   a. Does Satan still have power to do evil and provoke evil in people even though Jesus has been given all authority? Why or why not?

   b. How can a person appeal to Jesus' authority to overcome Satan's influence in their life?

2. Describe the similarities between these two passages:

> See to it that no one takes you captive through philosophy and empty deception, according to the tradition of men, according to the elementary principles of the world, rather than according to Christ. For in Him all the fullness of Deity dwells in bodily form, and in Him you have been made complete, and He is the head over all rule and authority; and in Him you were also circumcised with a circumcision made without hands, in the removal of the body of the flesh by the circumcision of Christ; having been buried with Him in baptism, in which you were also raised up with Him through faith in the working of God, who raised Him from the dead (Colossians 2:8-12).

> God, being rich in mercy, because of His great love with which He loved us, even when we were dead in our transgressions, made us alive together with Christ (by grace you have been saved), and raised us up with Him, and seated us with Him in the heavenly places in Christ Jesus, so that in the ages to come He might show the surpassing riches of His grace in kindness toward us in Christ Jesus (Ephesians 2:4-7).

In what practical ways should Jesus' power and authority over all (which are available to us in Him through faith) manifest themselves in our daily thoughts, words, and actions?

3. Read aloud the following passages.

   • "In the beginning God created the heavens and the earth" (Genesis 1:1).

   • "The LORD God formed man of dust from the ground, and breathed into his nostrils the breath of life; and man became a living being" (Genesis 2:7).

   • "The LORD God took the man and put him into the garden of Eden to cultivate it and keep it" (Genesis 2:15).

   • "God said, 'Let Us make man in Our image, according to Our likeness; and let them rule over the fish of the sea and over the birds of the sky and over the cattle and over all the earth, and over every creeping thing that creeps on the earth.' God created man in His own image, in the image of God He created him; male and female He created them. God blessed them; and God said to them, 'Be fruitful and multiply, and fill the earth, and subdue it; and rule over the fish of the sea and over the birds of the sky and over every living thing that moves on the earth' " (Genesis 1:26-28).

   • "What is man that You take thought of him, and the son of man that You care for him? Yet You have made him a little lower than God, and You crown him with glory and majesty! You make him to rule over the works of Your hands; You have put all things under his feet" (Psalm 8:4-6).

- "The heavens are the heavens of the LORD, but the earth He has given to the sons of men" (Psalm 115:16).

  a. What is the progression in these verses?

  b. In what way are we assigned to steward God's creation under His rule as King?

  c. People often associate the term *stewardship* with managing money. But according to these Scriptures, we are given the responsibility of stewarding much more. How can you steward your time, skills, and resources in order to advance God's kingdom agenda?

In Closing

As you end the group study today, pray together for the willingness to align your thoughts and actions under the Lord and His rightful rule. Perhaps some in the group would want to share a personal example of when they did or did not do that—and what the result was. Ask God for insight, discernment, and a daily dose of personal discipline to put Jesus' will above your own.

Before moving on to session 3, complete the On Your Own Between Sessions section below.

On Your Own Between Sessions

Far too many people come into God's kingdom with their old way of thinking and their old rules. They enter His kingdom holding allegiance to their former ruler, the flesh. Relying on how you were raised, what your friends say, what your flesh desires, or what the media and culture purports as positive is only going to stir up conflict with your new ruler, Christ the King. Just like you would experience conflict if your teenage kids were to bring their friends into your home and they all chose to abide by their rules and not yours.

The Power of Jesus' Names, page 53

1. What would happen if the above scenario with teenagers took place in your own home? How would you seek to address it?

    a. How does this give you insight into the heart of God when you live in His creation and yet act any way you choose?

    b. What specific step can you take this week in order to align your actions under Jesus' rightful rule over you?

2. Read Luke 12:31-32.

    a. What is the result of seeking Jesus' kingdom and His rulership over all?

    b. In what ways does this truth impact your emotions?

    c. Consider a time when you did not seek Christ's kingdom first. What was the result?

    d. What are some hesitations you feel when it comes to seeking Christ's kingdom and agenda above your own?

A lot of us are missing out on the things that God wants to do in our hearts, relationships, finances, jobs, and circumstances simply because we refuse to put God first in our thoughts, attitudes, and decisions. One of the reasons so many people remain defeated for so long is that they do not treat Jesus as King. It's true that the flesh will always seek to nullify Jesus' authority. It pushes back against His commands. But one way to overcome the flesh is to give Jesus permission to tell you what to do. Then obey Him. Let Jesus tell you what to do about alcohol, pornography, your tongue, heart, relationships, hope, and faith. Let His rule overrule your flesh, and you will be set free.

The Power of Jesus' Names, pages 54-55

3. Pray for insight into an area(s) of your life in which you need to experience more freedom and Jesus' power to overrule. Write it (or them) down. Ask God to give you the strength to put Jesus first so you can experience His power to overcome.

4. Do you believe God is able to overrule whatever it is you are facing? Why or why not?

Life Exercise: Participating in Jesus' Power

1. *Identify* one area in your life where you need more spiritual power. Examine how you are currently facing the situation.

2. *Consider* other ways you can react or respond and different steps you can take.

3. *Evaluate* how to proceed. Consider the connection between honoring Jesus as Lord and King and Him bestowing His power on you. How might you need to adjust your attitude toward Him?

4. *Choose* what you will do when this situation comes along this week.

5. *Learn.* As you put Jesus and His rule first, consider what you are learning from the process. Has anything changed in your circumstances? Have you experienced Jesus' power in the midst of your own emotions? Can you seek to make this way of thinking a pattern in your life?

Recommended Reading

In preparation for session 3, you may want to read chapters 4 and 5 of *The Power of Jesus' Names.*

PRIEST AND LAMB

Hebrews is one of the more difficult books of the Bible to comprehend. Most people consider it the second most difficult New Testament book to understand after Revelation. One of the reasons Hebrews can be so confusing is that the book was written with an assumption. That assumption is that its readers had a solid understanding of the Old Testament.

In the Old Testament, we see many sacrifices, symbols, regulations, and systems in place that contributed to the daily routine of people's lives. And while Jews living in the day that Hebrews was written would have been entirely familiar with all of this and more, most of us living today simply are not.

Many of us don't come from that background. We are not steeped in Old Testament tradition or theology, the sacrificial system, nor the biblical priesthood. As a result, it is unclear to many of us what Hebrews is even talking about.

If I were to summarize the main point and message of the book of Hebrews for you, I would do it in three words: Never give up. That's the bottom line of all the peculiar elements of this book.

Never give up.

This book was written to a group of believers who were severely struggling with throwing in the towel. They were tempted to walk away from the faith. They were tempted to give up or give in because life had become too hard. Living as a Christian in their culture had become too difficult. They faced persecution, pressure, challenges, and overwhelming odds on a daily basis. Life was hard. Which is why the author of Hebrews sought to remind them not to quit. Not to give in. Not to give up. Not to let their hearts, which had already grown weary, simply stop.

You might be able to identify with the audience of Hebrews. You might find yourself in dire situations and feel tempted to quit. It could be you are raising the question, "Why go on?" You feel that things will never change. It simply isn't going to get any better. You may think you will never find the victory you are looking for or discover the life you hope to live.

Even though we are Christians, go to church, say our prayers, and seek the Lord, there are times when each of us (if we're honest) feel tempted to give up. There are times when we are merely holding on by a thread and feeling as if one small thing could tip us over.

But the author of the book of Hebrews seeks to explain why you don't have to give up or give in. And it all hinges on one name of Jesus: Great High Priest.

The Power of Jesus' Names, pages 83-85

Video Teaching Notes

As you watch the video, use the spaces below to take notes. Some key points and quotes are provided here as reminders.

Teaching: Priest and Lamb

The role of priest in the Old Testament was to help the people through carrying out sacrifices for sin. Jesus came to fulfill both parts of this role—as the lamb (the sacrifice) and the priest (the mediator between God and man).

Jesus is the Great High Priest, after the order of Melchizedek. This makes Him unique among all priests.

The presence of the blood from the sacrificed lamb averted the wrath of God from sinful humanity for a certain time frame. After that time, the sacrifice would need to be repeated. But Jesus' sacrificial atonement on the cross has averted God's wrath against sin for all time.

Quotables

- The good news of the gospel is that when faith alone is placed in Christ alone as the Lamb of God, there is deliverance from sin.

- Your Great High Priest refreshes you after you come out of one battle and equips you for the battle you're getting ready to face. We're always coming out of one and going into another.

- Because our Great High Priest became a man (in the person of Jesus Christ), He can feel what we feel, hurt where we hurt, and understand what we are going through.

Video Group Discussion

Read the shaded verses together and answer the questions that follow.

> The blood shall be a sign for you on the houses where you live; and when I see the blood I will pass over you, and no plague will befall you to destroy you when I strike the land of Egypt (Exodus 12:13).

1. In order for the Israelites to be spared from what God had said He would do in killing all the firstborn in Egypt, they were instructed to take the blood of an unblemished lamb and paint it on the doorposts of their homes. When God came by each home, He would recognize the sacrifice and pass over. What would be the result?

The blood of the lamb was symbolic of the role of Christ in our lives. Describe how the Passover lamb foreshadows Jesus' role as the Lamb of God.

God is holy. God is just. He is not merely reactional when it comes to His response to sin. He doesn't just lose it and get mad. Rather, God's wrath is tied to His justice, and His justice is part of His nature.

The Power of Jesus' Names, page 63

2. What does God's justice demand with regard to sin in a person's life?

> It is impossible for the blood of bulls and goats to take away sins…Every priest stands daily ministering and offering time after time the same sacrifices, which can never take away sins; but He, having offered one sacrifice for sins for all time, sat down at the right hand of God, waiting from that time onward until His enemies be made a footstool for His feet. For by one offering He has perfected for all time those who are sanctified (Hebrews 10:4,11-14).

3. Describe the difference between the sacrifices the priests made in the Old Testament and the sacrifice Jesus made on the cross as the Lamb of God.

Do you believe that Jesus' sacrifice as the Lamb of God truly applies "for all time" as it states in verse 12? Why or why not? In what ways do we negate that truth through our actions or emotions?

4. Read aloud the following passages.

- "Knowing that you were not redeemed with perishable things like silver or gold from your futile way of life inherited from your forefathers, but with precious blood, as of a lamb unblemished and spotless, the blood of Christ" (1 Peter 1:18-19).

- "Clean out the old leaven so that you may be a new lump, just as you are in fact unleavened. For Christ our Passover also has been sacrificed" (1 Corinthians 5:7).

- "The next day he saw Jesus coming to him and said, 'Behold, the Lamb of God who takes away the sin of the world!'" (John 1:29).

- "He Himself is the propitiation for our sins; and not for ours only, but also for those of the whole world" (1 John 2:2).

- "God was in Christ reconciling the world to Himself, not counting their trespasses against them, and He has committed to us the word of reconciliation" (2 Corinthians 5:19).

    a. Describe the conjoining thread throughout these passages.

    b. How should the knowledge of Jesus' role as the Lamb of God provide you with peace and affect your decision making?

5. In the video, Dr. Evans notes three things Jesus accomplished as the Lamb and the Great High Priest. Take a moment to describe each one and explain how they should impact your life and choices.

    1. *Justification*

    2. *Redemption*

    3. *Propitiation*

Group Bible Exploration

Read the shaded passages together and answer the questions that follow.

> They overcame him because of the blood of the Lamb and because of the word of their testimony, and they did not love their life even when faced with death (Revelation 12:11).

1. Based on this passage, what does the blood of the Lamb give you the ability to do?

   a. Most of us consider the blood of the Lamb as the means for our eternal salvation, which is true. But we often neglect to realize the power of the Lamb in our everyday lives. Revelation 12:11 shows us how to activate the power of this name of Jesus. What is one thing we are to do in connection with the blood of the Lamb to gain access to Jesus' power?

   b. In what ways can you share the word of your testimony with others? Consider methods beyond writing out your testimony or giving a formal talk on what God has done in your life. Are there small, regular ways you can share your testimony on an ongoing basis?

   c. Take a moment and allow some group members to share the testimony of Jesus' power in their lives.

> This hope we have as an anchor of the soul, a hope both sure and steadfast and one which enters within the veil, where Jesus has entered as a forerunner for us, having become a high priest forever according to the order of Melchizedek (Hebrews 6:19-20).

2. What does it mean to have hope as an anchor for the soul?

   Hope is joyful expectation about the future. Hope is not concerned with where you are right now. Hope looks to where things are going to wind up. It always involves expectation. The high priesthood of Jesus Christ holds you steady while you wait with expectation. It keeps you grounded in the midst of the chaos you face.

The Power of Jesus' Names, page 91

a. On the scale below (with 10 being the highest), indicate your current level of hope regarding your future. (Be honest.)

1 5 10

b. Now think about your greatest concern or worry. Indicate on the scale below your current level of hope regarding this particular issue. (Again, be honest.)

1 5 10

c. With Jesus as your Great High Priest, your hope can and should be a 10. It is only when trust in Him wanes that this number drops. Describe how life might be different for you if you lived in an ongoing state of complete faith and a high level of hope.

> Since we have a great high priest who has passed through the heavens, Jesus the Son of God, let us hold fast our confession. For we do not have a high priest who cannot sympathize with our weaknesses, but One who has been tempted in all things as we are, yet without sin. Therefore let us draw near with confidence to the throne of grace, so that we may receive mercy and find grace to help in time of need (Hebrews 4:14-16).

3. In the excerpt at the start of this week's session, Dr. Evans reminded us that the book of Hebrews was written to a group of people who desperately wanted to give up. Throughout

the book, this name of Jesus (Great High Priest) serves as an encouragement to them (and us) to look to Jesus for help in times of need. Based on the passage above, what are two things Jesus can provide when you turn to Him?

-

-

a. Describe the difference between mercy and grace. In what ways do we need both in our lives?

b. How does knowing that your Great High Priest sympathizes with your weaknesses bring you comfort?

c. Have you ever judged someone harshly because you didn't understand his or her situation—only to change your attitude when you experienced a similar life challenge? If so, describe what happened.

d. How does Jesus' identification with our weaknesses and challenges in life provoke compassion in Him rather than judgment?

In Closing

As you close your time together today, encourage one another to find peace and courage in these two names of Jesus. Honesty in your struggles will help you become more willing to depend on Jesus. Awareness of the battle *is* half the battle.

Consider these words from Dr. Evans as you wrap up this session. Have a volunteer read them out loud to the group. Then take a moment to pray together.

> [Jesus] can sympathize. He understands. He feels what you feel. That's why He has so much compassion. And you and I can access that sympathy and compassion by drawing near to the throne of grace, where we receive mercy and grace to help us in our times of need. But we must take the step to draw near. We must move forward in confidence. If you have a long-distance relationship with Jesus, your Great High Priest, you will never get to witness His priesthood working on your behalf. If you are only a Sunday-morning Christian, you will never experience His priesthood helping you in your times of need. In order to see God intervene in your situations, you need to confidently approach Him through the relationship you have with Jesus, the Great High Priest. You've got to draw near.
>
> You should never walk away from God if you are hurting. You ought to run toward Him. It's not good to stay away. You must draw near. In fact, He may even allow what you are going through to go on longer because He is trying to get you to draw near to Him. It's only as you come closer to God through the access of the Great High Priest that you can then access the grace and mercy you need.
>
> Since Jesus occupies a throne, He can dispense divine favor (grace). And since He is our sympathetic High Priest, He can simultaneously dispense compassion (mercy). Draw near, and in so doing, you will find strength to keep going. You will find deliverance (Hebrews 7:23-25). You will find peace. You will find the Great High Priest, who will give you the help you need.
>
> *The Power of Jesus' Names*, pages 95-96

Before moving on to session 4, complete the On Your Own Between Sessions section below.

On Your Own Between Sessions

1. Read the following passages from the book of Revelation.

   - "I saw between the throne (with the four living creatures) and the elders a Lamb standing, as if slain, having seven horns and seven eyes, which are the seven Spirits of God, sent out into all the earth" (5:6).

   - "When He had taken the book, the four living creatures and the twenty-four elders fell down before the Lamb, each one holding a harp and golden bowls full of incense, which are the prayers of the saints" (5:8).

- "I looked, and I heard the voice of many angels around the throne and the living creatures and the elders; and the number of them was myriads of myriads, and thousands of thousands, saying with a loud voice, 'Worthy is the Lamb that was slain to receive power and riches and wisdom and might and honor and glory and blessing.' And every created thing which is in heaven and on the earth and under the earth and on the sea, and all things in them, I heard saying, 'To Him who sits on the throne, and to the Lamb, be blessing and honor and glory and dominion forever and ever.' And the four living creatures kept saying, 'Amen.' And the elders fell down and worshiped" (5:11-14).

- "I saw when the Lamb broke one of the seven seals, and I heard one of the four living creatures saying as with a voice of thunder, 'Come'" (6:1).

- "After these things I looked, and behold, a great multitude which no one could count, from every nation and all tribes and peoples and tongues, standing before the throne and before the Lamb, clothed in white robes, and palm branches were in their hands" (7:9).

- "These will wage war against the Lamb, and the Lamb will overcome them, because He is Lord of lords and King of kings, and those who are with Him are the called and chosen and faithful" (17:14).

This is no ordinary lamb. This is the Lamb of God, who takes away the sins of the world and is worthy of our worship. He sits on the throne. He wages victorious warfare. He receives power, might, and honor. This is the DNA of the Lamb of God.

The Power of Jesus' Names, page 79

a. Compare and contrast this insight into the Lamb of God with what is frequently thought of in reference to this name.

b. How does understanding the power of the Lamb give you courage as you face your daily circumstances?

Satan is no mild enemy. He has claws. He has strength. His jaws can crush you. He is deceptive and comes at you through a variety of attempts to take you off track from living out your kingdom destiny for God. It is only when you activate the power of Jesus' blood as your covering and as your spiritual weaponry that you will walk in victory.

Understand this name. Worship this name. Apply this name. Honor this name. It is in this name that you will find protection, power, and strength. Worthy is the Lamb.

The Power of Jesus' Names, page 80

2. List some practical and specific ways you can worship, apply, and honor this name of Jesus.

3. Read Hebrews 5:5-10.

   a. What does this passage teach us about suffering?

   b. Do you try to avoid or embrace personal suffering when it happens? What might be the result if you sought to learn lessons of obedience in your suffering (as Jesus did in the role of our Great High Priest)?

4. Read Romans 5:3-5.

   a. List three positive results that can arise from difficulties in your life.

      1.

      2.

      3.

b. In what ways might you abort the process of achieving these positive results when you face trials or challenges?

Life Exercise: Applying Jesus' Power in Pain

This week, be intentional in seeking Jesus' power when you face a painful situation on any level. It could be emotionally painful, physically painful, relationally painful, etc.

Spend some time meditating on the power Jesus provides as both the mighty Lamb who enables you to overcome and the sympathizing Great High Priest who provides you direct access to the throne of God.

As you continually think it over in your mind, it will become more natural to use this mindset when something painful happens. Don't wait until you are in the midst of a hard situation to consider what to do. Plan to shift your thinking now, looking for comfort in Christ and power from Him. Then when difficulties do arise, you will have an automatic and powerful tool to usher you through the situation, developing your spiritual muscles along the way.

Recommended Reading

In preparation for session 4, you may want to read chapters 7 and 12 of *The Power of Jesus' Names*.

SESSION 4

I Am and the Word

We read in John 1:14 how Jesus took on flesh and "dwelt among us." The term *dwelt* in this verse means "pitched His tent." Literally, the verse reads, "The Word became flesh, and [tented] among us." Another synonym for *tent* is *tabernacle*. The audience to whom John was writing would have understood what he meant when He said the Word became flesh and became a living tabernacle among them. They knew the meaning because they knew the history of the Israelites in the wilderness. They knew that a tabernacle was set up with a unique, special place within called the Holy of Holies. In this area of the tabernacle sat the Ark of the Covenant. On top of this ark were two golden cherubim that oversaw the mercy seat, where God's presence dwelt. Inside the ark rested the two tablets containing the Ten Commandments (Exodus 25:10-22).

Picture this: The glory of God was on top of the chest, while the Ten Commandments were within the chest under the mercy seat. And all this rested within the confines of the Holy of Holies in the tabernacle in the wilderness.

This is the scene John references when introducing the concept that Jesus "tented" among us. He came into a sin-soaked world, a wilderness of souls, bringing the presence of God through His own mercy. He came to bring life where life was not found. He did it for people back then, and He still does it for us today. Which is why I can say that it doesn't matter how dry your wilderness is…or how many thorns and thistles have grown in your circumstances…or how many Canaanites, Hittites, Amorites, or Jebusites have surrounded you. It doesn't matter, because a tent has been pitched right in the middle of your wilderness existence. And that tent is the Word made flesh.

Jesus walked the streets in Israel. He talked. He ate. He did all the things humans do, but He did them as the manifested Word—the revelation of God. Which is why we read in John 1:14 that we "saw His glory, glory as of the only begotten from the Father." Notice that this verse says "only begotten," which suggests He is uniquely one of a kind. There is none like Him. There has never been, nor will there ever be, another Jesus.

The Power of Jesus' Names, pages 229-230

Video Teaching Notes

As you watch the video, use the spaces below to take notes. Some key points and quotes are provided here as reminders.

Teaching 1: I Am

When Jesus identified Himself as I Am, He created great division and resistance toward Him among the Jews. In claiming this name as His own, He let everyone know that He truly is God.

Jesus spoke to the Jewish leaders of His day, telling them not just to believe the words He said, but also to believe the signs and miracles He performed to back up those words (John 10:37-38). When Jesus raised Lazarus from the grave, He demonstrated His identity as I Am.

Jesus can still raise the dead today. It could be that you have experienced a death in your hopes, relationships, or another area of your life. The great I Am has the power to bring back to life what you thought was completely over.

Teaching 2: The Word

The Greek term for *word* is *logos*. It refers to an impersonal force and the sum total of all knowledge. John merged the concept of logos with the personal nature of God when he wrote, "The Word became flesh" (John 1:14).

As the Word, Jesus communicates on behalf of God the Father. He explains the Father not only through His actions while on earth, but also through His attributes and ongoing actions.

Abiding in the written Word of God while keeping your mind focused on the living Word opens up a funnel through which God can deliver His power to you.

Quotables

- Jesus didn't keep Martha and Mary *from* the pain, but His I Am-ness joined them *in* the pain.

- Maybe your resurrection hasn't occurred because you haven't moved the stone. Demonstrate that you believe Jesus is the I Am. Do what He has told you to do. Act in obedience, and let's see what resurrection He brings in your life and in your circumstances.

- Jesus Christ perfectly communicates the heart, the mind, and the Spirit of God.

- God moved into our neighborhood in the person of Jesus Christ. He "tented" among us.

Video Group Discussion

1. The teaching on Jesus as the Word was filmed at the location of the synagogue in Nazareth where Jesus would have read from Isaiah 61. The building was constructed upon the ruins and remains of that synagogue, which no longer exists. But the truths Jesus read that day remain as strong now as they were then. Take a moment to read Luke 4:16-21, where Jesus quotes from Isaiah. List the five different descriptions Jesus says He came to fulfill.

   1.

   2.

   3.

   4.

   5.

Read the shaded verses together and answer the questions that follow.

> In the beginning was the Word, and the Word was with God, and the Word was God (John 1:1).

2. What does this verse tell us about the existence of Jesus prior to being born on earth? How does this truth bring you comfort as you face challenges that arise in your life?

3. When Dr. Evans introduces the name I Am in the video at what is believed to be the tomb of Lazarus in Bethany, he starts out by referring to the many variations of this name. Read the following passages from the book of John together and describe in your own words what each name means.

- "I am the bread of life; he who comes to Me will not hunger, and he who believes in Me will never thirst" (6:35).

- "I am the Light of the world; he who follows Me will not walk in the darkness, but will have the Light of life" (8:12).

- "Truly, truly, I say to you, I am the door of the sheep" (10:7).

- "I am the good shepherd; the good shepherd lays down His life for the sheep… I am the good shepherd, and I know My own and My own know Me" (10:11,14).

- "I am the resurrection and the life; he who believes in Me will live even if he dies" (11:25).

- "I am the way, and the truth, and the life; no one comes to the Father but through Me" (14:6).

- "I am the true vine, and My Father is the vinedresser…I am the vine, you are the branches; he who abides in Me and I in him, he bears much fruit, for apart from Me you can do nothing" (15:1,5).

4. In the video, Dr. Evans connects the act of faith in obeying what Jesus has said ("Remove the stone" [John 11:39]) with accessing the power to reverse the situation on hand (raising the dead). In what ways have you experienced Jesus' power in your own life, as tied to a specific action of faith on your part?

   a. Have you ever downplayed the role obedience (acts of faith) plays in God's willingness to move on your behalf? Do you think our current Christian culture downplays it? Why or why not?

   b. List three areas in your life where you believe God is asking you to step out in faith. (They can be small.)

     1.

     2.

     3.

Take a moment to pray as a group, asking Jesus to infuse each person with the courage, belief, and confidence to move forward in faith where they have been led. Ask for Jesus' power to be made manifest in restoring whatever has been lost or diminished in each person's life.

Group Bible Exploration

1. Read John 8:48-59. (Have a group member look up the passage and read it aloud.) Then have another group member (or multiple group members) read aloud what Dr. Evans writes concerning Jesus' revelation of the name I Am.

The name I Am shows up in the midst of a heated discussion. Not long before, Jesus had forgiven the adulterous woman and driven away a number of angry, hypocritical, judgmental men who sought to stone her. His miracles of healing and driving out demons had given Him a reputation by this time. Jesus was someone to be reckoned with, yet not everyone knew how to place Him. Was He a good man doing good things? Was He of the devil using demonic powers? Was He…God?

Consider for a moment how Jesus must have felt during this heated discussion that we read about in John 8:48-59. Jews encircled Him and pounded Him with questions and accusations. Words quickly became harsh. Some accused Him of having a demon. To which Jesus unloaded a soliloquy of sorts, a somewhat personal reflection that was also for the benefit of others. After all, Jesus was speaking to those He came to redeem. The sins He would carry on the cross were their sins. Not only that, but the blood that coursed through their veins was blood He created. The skin that held their organs in place was skin He held together. The air they breathed was air He made and preserved each and every day. It was His genius which had prepared a place where humanity could live, food could be produced, and regeneration could occur. It was His strength that held the stars at bay so they would not tumble too closely and destroy the planet. His energy infused the sun. He gave life to each person standing there, even the ones nodding in agreement that He might have a demon in Him.

It's one thing to be insulted by someone who doesn't know you. Maybe you can identify. If someone you barely know on social media or a casual acquaintance mocks you, that's one level of pain. But when the very people you sustain—either through caregiving, provision, or some other way—insult you, it's difficult to contain the feelings of outright pain.

No doubt Jesus' words came peppered with an extra bit of spice when He rebuked His accusers that day. It's surprising that He didn't just raise His hand and make them all fall instantly to the ground. How dare they even insinuate that the one who gave them the ability to speak is less than they are, as lowly and unrighteous as a demon.

But Jesus exercised power in His self-control. I would have loved to have seen the look in His eyes and hear the lengthened breath He took when He replied, "I do not have a demon." Perhaps He looked down at that point. Perhaps He looked up. Perhaps He stared right into the souls of His accusers. Whatever the case, I imagine He could have pierced the core of the earth with His gaze when He continued, "I honor My Father, and you dishonor Me" (John 8:49).

Jesus continued the dialogue a bit longer. Accusations kept coming. His responses showed restraint coupled with intentionality. Until, ultimately, He left it all on the table. The Jews around Him mocked Him by jesting, "You are not yet fifty years old, and have You seen Abraham?" And He did not hold back. His reply revealed all. I can almost hear His voice softening, growing patient like a parent with a child who simply will not understand. "Truly, truly, I say to you, before Abraham was born, I am" (verses 57-58).

He knew that statement would end the conversation. And, in fact, it did.

The Power of Jesus' Names, pages 122-124

a. Share your thoughts on the range of emotions Jesus may have felt during His revelation of the name I Am.

b. In what ways do we likewise insult the totality of who Jesus is as the great I Am when we question His will, leading, or calling in our lives?

> Jesus, knowing all the things that were coming upon Him, went forth and said to them, "Whom do you seek?" They answered Him, "Jesus the Nazarene." He said to them, "I am He." And Judas also, who was betraying Him, was standing with them. So when He said to them, "I am He," they drew back and fell to the ground (John 18:4-6).

2. Why do you think the soldiers who were with Judas fell to the ground when Jesus told them His name and who He was?

a. What does this tell us about the power of Jesus to overcome opposition or a direct challenge?

b. Seeing the patience of Jesus in this passage, knowing what was about to come upon Him, helps us gain insight into the character God wants each of us to have. In what ways can this example of Jesus' restraint teach us how to handle conflict or act in a way that reflects trust in God's sovereign plan?

3. From John 1:1,14, we discover that the Word is...

preexistent

coexistent

self-existent

tangibly existent

self-contained

self-evident

Describe each of these terms in your own contemporary wording as if you were explaining the concept of the Word's existence to an unbeliever.

He is clothed with a robe dipped in blood, and His name is called The Word of God (Revelation 19:13).

4. Share what the name Word of God means to you personally as it relates to Jesus.

   a. In what ways does understanding Jesus as the living Word of God bring life and depth to your reading of the written Word of God?

   b. Is abiding in the written Word of God a form of abiding in the living Word of God? Why or why not? What does *abide* mean to you?

In Closing

As you end the group study today, spend some time considering the strength and vulnerability Jesus displayed in revealing the name I Am. What personal lessons can you take from this in order to reflect His character more closely? Take a moment to pray for everyone in the group and ask that God will grant each of you a new level of spiritual maturity as you reflect on these two powerful names of Jesus.

Before moving on to session 5, complete the On Your Own Between Sessions section below.

On Your Own Between Sessions

1. Jesus said, "While I am in the world, I am the Light of the world" (John 9:5). When Jesus went away, He sent a Helper. Describe this Helper (the Holy Spirit) and how you seek to interact with Him in your own life. List three key attributes of the Holy Spirit. (You may want to reference the following passages: John 14:26; 1 Corinthians 12:4-7; Galatians 5:22-23.)

   1.

   2.

   3.

2. Read Hebrews 4:12. Take a moment to describe the various qualities of God's Word and how they directly relate to Jesus.

    a. *Living*

    b. *Active*

    c. *Piercing*

    d. *Able to judge* (discerning)

3. Reflect on the Word. How seriously do you take the Word of God? How do you engage it on a regular basis in order for it to be living, active, piercing, and discerning in your own life?

Take some serious time to mull over this—to pray, to feel, to be convicted, and to let the attributes found in God's Word (through the living Word) begin to resonate more fully in you. Let the Holy Spirit guide your emotions. Ask yourself, "How would my days and hours be different if I took seriously the living and written Word?" What would happen to your work life and home life if you let the abiding words of Christ infiltrate all your conversations, decisions, and actions?

Life Exercise: Abiding

One way to come to know Jesus more personally is to connect with His name Word of God more regularly. You can do this through reading the written Word and asking God to reveal to you His will, wisdom, and insights.

Set aside time each day over the course of the next week to seek Jesus in Scripture. Choose a passage and then read it every day for seven days. Each day before you read it, pray that God will prepare your heart to hear from Him. Take time to write down the various insights He gives you. Revisiting the same passage offers you the opportunity to abide more fully in the written Word, increasing your ability to hear from Him regarding the meaning and application of His Word.

Recommended Reading

In preparation for session 5, you may want to read chapter 10 of *The Power of Jesus' Names*.

MESSIAH AND SAVIOR

When Andrew said they had found the Messiah in John 1:41, he was talking about someone he had been looking for. We know this by Andrew's use of the word *found*. If a person says they have found something, implied within that statement is that they were looking for something. In fact, it wasn't only Andrew who had been looking for the anointed one. It was all of Israel. The entire Old Testament was written in anticipation of the one to come who would fulfill the role of Messiah. This is known as the messianic hope. It is impossible to fully understand the Old Testament unless you also understand the messianic hope. Generation after generation after generation after generation looked forward to this promised person of God who would come not only for the Israelites, but who would come to impact the entire world through the establishment of the kingdom of God on earth. The person they looked for was the Messiah, known in Greek (the language of the New Testament) as the Christ.

Luke 24:25-27 gives us the culmination of that long walk on the Emmaus road, when Jesus spent time with a couple of His downtrodden followers after His death and resurrection (although they did not immediately recognize Him). It is in these verses that we see Jesus revisiting the Old Testament to explain who He was. These followers were discouraged, after all, because they had expected Him to deliver Israel from Roman oppression (verse 21), but instead they had witnessed His death, not anticipating His resurrection. So as Jesus walked with them, He returned to the Old Testament to reveal who He was. In doing so, He referenced the Christ.

> He said to them, "O foolish men and slow of heart to believe in all that the prophets have spoken! Was it not necessary for the Christ to suffer these things

and to enter into His glory?" Then beginning with Moses and with all the prophets, He explained to them the things concerning Himself in all the Scriptures (verses 25-27).

The whole Old Testament, while not using Jesus' personal name, anticipates Jesus' person coming as the Messiah (or Christ). For example, in Genesis 3:15, we read that the woman would have a "seed" through which would come this Messiah. Now, whenever we talk about the seed for a baby, we are referencing the sperm provided by a man. Yet, in this case it is written that the woman has the seed. This is because there would be no man involved in creating a child born to a virgin. The Messiah would come through the seed of a woman, which would connect with the Spirit of God Himself.

Genesis 3:15 is our introduction to the one who would come to fulfill the role of the anointed one. As we move on through the Old Testament, we see how God set up an entire system of sacrifices in anticipation of the coming Messiah. He set up a whole festival arrangement looking toward the arrival of the Messiah. He even made certain promises to Israel—and through Israel, to the whole world—which would be fulfilled by the reign of the Messiah.

We also run across a number of prayers in the Bible which look forward to the coming of the Messiah. We read sermons about how justice would rule at the coming of the Messiah. The central message of the Old Testament revolves around anticipating the one who was to come and embody the messianic hope.

Thus, in the context of how the Israelites understood the Messiah and His role, when Andrew said they had "found the Messiah" (John 1:41), he was saying they had found the one about whom the entire Old Testament had prophesied and spoken. Jesus is the Christ, the anointed one from God who fulfills the promises put forth by God for the world.

The Power of Jesus' Names, pages 183-186

Video Teaching Notes

As you watch the video, use the spaces that follow to take notes. Some key points and quotes are provided here as reminders.

Teaching 1: Messiah

The entire Old Testament was written in anticipation of the coming Messiah. The concept of the Messiah was birthed in the promise that there would be one from the seed of a woman who would defeat Satan and fulfill the promises of God to His people. The role of Messiah involved three official distinctions for Jesus: prophet, priest, and king.

Teaching 2: Savior

Every problem in our lives is related to sin—either our own sin, someone else's sin that has affected us, or an environment contaminated by sin.

God's judgment on sin was satisfied by the sacrificial birth and death of His Son. When we place our faith in Him, God cancels our debt, so we are now debt free before a holy God.

Jesus' role as Savior addresses all levels of what we truly need, because it is in addressing the spiritual need for forgiveness of sin that we find access to the strength, authority, and power required to overcome sin's impact and influence in our lives.

Quotables

- Jesus brings the fulfillment of God's promises into history.

- To have Jesus Christ as your Messiah is not merely to have a Savior who takes you to heaven, but also to have an anointed one whose job it is to bring the Word of God, the presence of God, and the rule of God to you while you are living on earth. But that only takes place if He is your identity.

- The name Jesus means "deliverer" or "rescuer," and God's eternal Son, Jesus Christ, came to rescue people from the consequences of sin.

Video Group Discussion

1. Dr. Evans introduces the concept that Christ (or Messiah; the names are used interchangeably) is not Jesus' last name. Rather, this name indicates certain roles and responsibilities

that Jesus fulfills. Briefly describe each role in your own words and how it relates to people in our contemporary culture.

    a. *Prophet*

    b. *Priest*

    c. *King*

2. In the video, Dr. Evans explains how the concept of the Messiah reaches all the way back to the beginning of time, and the entire Old Testament was written in a context of awaiting and seeking the coming Messiah. We live in a time where we are now awaiting the return of Christ to set up His kingdom rule and usher in eternity. Compare and contrast the Old Testament's awaiting of the Messiah with our current culture's awaiting of the returning King.

What are three practical ways we can demonstrate more openly and regularly that we are awaiting our returning Lord Jesus Christ?

    1.

    2.

    3.

3. In the video, Dr. Evans says that "a little bit of sin can wreak havoc—and has wreaked havoc—on our lives and our world." He then goes on to explain that not only did Jesus die so that we can have forgiveness from sin, but He also died so that we can have freedom from sin's power in our everyday lives. He refers to this in his writing as the "scope and content of

the gospel." In your own words, describe the difference between the "scope" and the "content" of the gospel.

    a. Give a biblical example of someone who was delivered from the power of sin's impact on their life.

    b. In what ways should we engage this aspect of Jesus' name (Savior) more fully (that is, as deliverance from the daily power of sin's pull and impact on our lives)?

4. The video portion on the name Savior was filmed in the Church of the Holy Sepulchre in Jerusalem, which many believe is the general location of Golgotha, where Jesus was crucified. This location was originally outside the city walls of Jerusalem, but approximately ten years after His death, a third wall was built to surround Jerusalem—and now this area is inside the walls. This is a fitting picture of Jesus' death ushering us into the presence of a holy God, from whom we had at one point been separated by sin. Take a moment to read Hebrews 4:16 aloud. Recall what Jesus' death has given each of us by way of our relationship with God.

Group Bible Exploration

1. Both Matthew 1 and Luke 3 describe the lineage of Jesus, but from different perspectives. Why is it important to know the ancestry of both His mother and earthly father?

2. Have someone (or multiple people) in the group read aloud the first chapter of Hebrews. Then list the names of Jesus you find in the passage (including descriptive terms or attributes).

3. Read aloud the following verses, which describe Jesus' role as Christ (the Messiah).

- "Jesus said to him, 'I am the way, and the truth, and the life; no one comes to the Father but through Me'" (John 14:6).

- "There is one God, and one mediator also between God and men, the man Christ Jesus" (1 Timothy 2:5).

- "He had to be made like His brethren in all things, so that He might become a merciful and faithful high priest in things pertaining to God, to make propitiation for the sins of the people. For since He Himself was tempted in that which He has suffered, He is able to come to the aid of those who are tempted" (Hebrews 2:17-18).

- "Since we have a great high priest who has passed through the heavens, Jesus the Son of God, let us hold fast our confession. For we do not have a high priest who cannot sympathize with our weaknesses, but One who has been tempted in all things as we are, yet without sin. Therefore let us draw near with confidence to the throne of grace, so that we may receive mercy and find grace to help in time of need" (Hebrews 4:14-16).

- "Being designated by God as a high priest according to the order of Melchizedek" (Hebrews 5:10).

  a. What is the overall theme of these verses?

  b. Why is it important to live intentionally in light of the truths evident in these passages?

  c. In what ways do these verses give us a glimpse into the compassionate, personal side of Jesus?

4. Read aloud the following passages.

- "Accept one another, just as Christ also accepted us to the glory of God" (Romans 15:7).

- "All of you who were baptized into Christ have clothed yourselves with Christ" (Galatians 3:27).

- "Whatever things were gain to me, those things I have counted as loss for the sake of Christ. More than that, I count all things to be loss in view of the surpassing value of knowing Christ Jesus my Lord, for whom I have suffered the loss of all things, and count them but rubbish so that I may gain Christ" (Philippians 3:7-8).

- "The mystery which has been hidden from the past ages and generations, but has now been manifested to His saints, to whom God willed to make known what is the riches of the glory of this mystery among the Gentiles, which is Christ in you, the hope of glory" (Colossians 1:26-27).

- "You have died and your life is hidden with Christ in God" (Colossians 3:3).

   a. What does it mean to "clothe" yourself with Christ?

   b. How should knowing, abiding in, and being hidden in Christ affect your own character qualities and attributes?

   c. Choose one thing you are going to do this week that will visibly demonstrate being clothed and hidden in Christ and knowing Him in a more intimate, abiding manner. For example, you might seek to have greater grace or patience with others. Be creative in what you choose, and then ask God to give you the power of Christ to follow through.

Recommended Reading

In preparation for session 6, you may want to read chapter 2 of *The Power of Jesus' Names*.

SESSION 6

ALPHA AND OMEGA

One of the first things we were taught when we started school, or even before then, was the alphabet. Parents, grandparents, and teachers seek to teach young children the alphabet as early as their first year of life. When I was growing up, we had songs that helped us memorize it. Today, there are a variety of games, toys, and videos little ones can interact with that will help them learn not only the letters, but also the sounds of each letter.

The reason why learning the alphabet is such an emphasized part of childhood is because knowing A to Z serves as the foundation upon which we can understand all words. Words depend on letters. Letters make up words. These words then comprise our thoughts, and the communication of those thoughts becomes the bedrock for all knowledge…

Because we know how important language and words are, we will often use the phrase "from A to Z" to indicate the fullness of a task or topic. This isn't merely referring to the letters in the alphabet. Rather, the phrase references the completeness of whatever point is being made.

The reason why the alphabet is so critical is because letters matter, words matter, thoughts matter, and knowledge matters.

Now, what "A to Z" is in the English language, "alpha and omega" is in Greek. *Alpha* is the first letter of the Greek alphabet, and *omega* is the last. When Jesus lived on earth, He lived in a Greek-speaking world. He understood the significance of *alpha* and *omega*. Just as "A to Z" signifies the completeness of communication, fullness of knowledge, and clarity of thought, the phrase "alpha and omega" symbolized the same for the culture in which Jesus lived. Thus, when He says He is the Alpha and Omega, He is declaring that He Himself is the complete knowledge base for all life. He is the entirety of all information. He is the answer to all questions. He is the sufficiency of all communication. He is the sum total of all that can be totaled.

Jesus followed up His claim to the name of Alpha and Omega by further identifying the scope of His existence and being. He did this by adding that He is "the first and the last" (Revelation 22:13). Essentially, no letter comes before Him, and no letter comes after Him. He is the first, the last, and everything in between.

The Power of Jesus' Names, pages 29-31

Video Teaching Notes

As you watch the video, use the spaces below to take notes. Some key points and quotes are provided here as reminders.

Teaching: Alpha and Omega

Jesus keeps His promises. He will take you to the finish line—the finish line of life, the finish line of ministry, the finish line of circumstances.

We have a great cloud of witnesses around us (Hebrews 12:1) who walked by faith in Jesus Christ, and He brought them to His intended purposes for them. Knowing that Jesus finishes what He starts brings stability and strength in areas such as…

emotional well-being

personal development

relational needs

living out your purpose

raising children

understanding grace

overcoming temptation

Quotables

- Jesus is the comprehensive statement, reflection, and manifestation of God.

- Jesus Christ is sufficient for all of life.

- Fixing your eyes on Jesus doesn't mean you won't have any challenges. It doesn't mean you won't have any problems. It means that the crucifixion of Friday becomes the resurrection of Sunday in your own life. God can take messes and create miracles.

Video Group Discussion

1. We encounter a variety of starts without finishes in our lives. In what ways does knowing and trusting that Jesus finishes everything He starts bring you comfort and confidence?

2. In what ways might we hinder the process of Jesus finishing what He started in our lives— particularly in our spiritual development or in living out the destiny He has chosen for us?

3. In the video, Dr. Evans notes that Jesus is not only the first and the last, but He is also the sum total of everything in between. He emphasizes the necessity of each part of the English alphabet, not just the beginning and the end. Take a moment to come up with as many words as you can by only using the first and last letters of the alphabet:

    Forming words when only using the first and last letters of the alphabet doesn't come easy. But once you start adding all the letters in between them, the options are endless.

    Far too often in our culture today, we use Jesus' name at the beginning of the convocation or in the benediction but leave Him—and His viewpoint—out of the "in between." Why is it important that Jesus be brought to bear on all aspects of your life, not just the start or finish?

4. When Peter attempted to walk on water, he became overwhelmed by the storm raging around him. That's when he took his eyes off Jesus. What happened when Peter chose to look elsewhere? (See Matthew 14:25-31.)

    a. What does it mean to fix your eyes on something or someone, as compared to glancing at them?

    b. How can the lesson Peter learned on the water guide you in your own difficult circumstances?

Group Bible Exploration

Read the shaded verses together and answer the questions that follow.

> This is what the Lord, the King of Israel and its Redeemer, the Lord of Armies, says: I am the first and I am the last. There is no God but me (Isaiah 44:6 csb).

> Listen to Me, O Jacob, even Israel whom I called; I am He, I am the first, I am also the last (Isaiah 48:12).

1. These verses give us insight into the origin of the concept "first and last." Before Jesus came to earth, God already referred to Himself in these terms. We often attach the words "first and last" primarily to Jesus, but what do these verses about God the Father reveal to you about Jesus as well?

Why is it important to have an expanded view of Jesus' names with regard to the triune nature of God?

> In Him all the fullness of Deity dwells in bodily form, and in Him you have been made complete, and He is the head over all rule and authority (Colossians 2:9-10).

2. Since all of God resides in all of Jesus, and we are made complete in Him when we are saved by faith in Christ, how much of what we need to live out the victorious Christian life do we already have?

What prevents you from accessing or using His provision in your life?

> He is also head of the body, the church; and He is the beginning, the firstborn from the dead, so that He Himself will come to have first place in everything (Colossians 1:18).

3. What are some practical ways you can give Christ "first place" in everything?

Look up and read the following verses together. Write down what each one says about putting God first.

a. Matthew 6:33

b. Exodus 20:3

c. Proverbs 3:9-10

> I am confident of this very thing, that He who began a good work in you will perfect it until the day of Christ Jesus (Philippians 1:6).

4. What does this passage mean to you personally?

a. God's faithfulness to perfect the good work He started in you is a promise. What can you do to cooperate with the process?

b. How does cooperating with the process of maturity and development enable that process to move forward more quickly and effectively?

c. Have you ever felt disappointed, slighted, or angry with God because of where you are in your life? Have you ever felt like you should be further along in your spiritual development? If so, take a moment to share that experience and what you have learned—or are learning—from it.

In Closing

As you end the group study today, pray together for strength and wisdom on seeking Jesus first in everything. Ask Jesus for the courage to put Him first, no matter what. Then talk about ways you could encourage or remind one another to look to Jesus (His perspective and His will) in all you do or say.

On Your Own Between Sessions

1. Read the following verses. What do they tell you about the comprehensive nature of Jesus?

   - "With a view to an administration suitable to the fullness of the times, that is, the summing up of all things in Christ, things in the heavens and things on the earth" (Ephesians 1:10).

   - "Far above all rule and authority and power and dominion, and every name that is named, not only in this age but also in the one to come" (Ephesians 1:21).

   - "He is the image of the invisible God, the firstborn of all creation" (Colossians 1:15).

   - "He is before all things, and in Him all things hold together" (Colossians 1:17).

   - "It was the Father's good pleasure for all the fullness to dwell in Him" (Colossians 1:19).

   - "In whom are hidden all the treasures of wisdom and knowledge" (Colossians 2:3).

   - "In Him all the fullness of Deity dwells in bodily form" (Colossians 2:9).

   - "A renewal in which there is no distinction between Greek and Jew, circumcised and uncircumcised, barbarian, Scythian, slave and freeman, but Christ is all, and in all" (Colossians 3:11).

   a. List five distinct attributes of Jesus you learn from these passages:

      1.

      2.

      3.

4.

5.

b. Now, take a moment to apply each of the five attributes to a specific concern or challenge you have in your life. For example:

"He is before all things"

Attribute: Jesus comes first

Application: My days seem to get away from me with the busyness of life.
Putting Jesus first in my thoughts and actions (spending time in His Word,
praying, etc.) will help me align my priorities for the rest of the day.

1.

2.

3.

4.

5.

2. Based on an understanding of the completeness of Jesus as Alpha and Omega, we ought to integrate His perspective into the totality of our life choices. Yet we often relegate Jesus to a Sunday morning service or small group Bible study—or a prayer here and there. Let's consider the reasons (emotions and convictions) you may have for relying on yourself when making decisions in your daily life. Then contrast them with the reasons you should have for including Jesus in all things.

Reasons to Rely on Yourself	Reasons to Rely on Jesus
•	•
•	•
•	•
•	•
•	•

Every single part of your life and mind is to be connected, plugged into, and in sync with Jesus Christ. He is the revelation of God from heaven to earth. His job was and is to bring the truth of heaven to bear on our lives on earth. What Jesus says, goes. At least that's how it should be.

The Power of Jesus' Names, page 36

3. What practical steps can you take this week to get entirely in sync with Jesus in every part of your life? Consider one or two specific things you can do to align your life under Him.

•

•

a. In your own words, what does Dr. Evans mean when he says, "His job was and is to bring the truth of heaven to bear on our lives on earth"?

b. What can you expect the outcome to be when you integrate Jesus into the sum total of your thoughts, words, and actions?

Life Exercise: Meditating Daily

This week, read the following excerpt from *The Power of Jesus' Names* once or twice daily. Meditate on different aspects of the concept highlighted in this excerpt each day. Take time to write down your thoughts in response to this daily reading.

Friend, I understand that you are probably tired right now. In Scripture, this type of tired is known as being "weary" or "losing heart." Life may not be working in your favor, as you see it. Sure, it could be your fault why it hasn't. But it could also be someone else's fault. Or it could be a combination of both. Regardless of the reason, the result is the same: You are tired. You are worn out. Your hope has waned, and your fervency has fizzled. But what the author of Hebrews is trying to tell you in this passage [Hebrews 12:1-3] is that if you are tired, you still need to keep going.

Even though things are rough right now, don't quit.

You have a race to finish—a figurative race of living the kingdom life for the glory of God and the good of yourself and others. And even though you may have gotten sidelined along the way or detoured by heeding human wisdom, Jesus can set you back on that racetrack and help you finish strong.

The author of Hebrews knew he wasn't writing to perfect people. He was writing to people marred by sin and failure and filled with regret. Flawed people who were just plain tired and wanted to quit. He knew all that, which is why he prodded them and goaded them to keep on going. And how were they (and you) to do that? By fixing their eyes on the one who knows how to both start and finish things—the Alpha and the Omega, the beginning and the end.

You have the power to keep going because Jesus has the power to both start and finish whatever it is you might face. He is the origin and completion of your faith walk. What you need to do is change your focus. You need to get back on track. Run the race set before you. And the way you do that is by focusing your eyes on Jesus. Become fixated with Him.

The Power of Jesus' Names, pages 38-39

In Closing

As you end this group study, remember to do the following:

1. Access the power of Jesus through intimately knowing and abiding in His names.

2. Rather than trying to solve problems on your own, let go and let Jesus step in with His grace and greatness.

3. Submit to Jesus' authority in your life as Lord and King. He is in control of your circumstances. He is not surprised by them. They serve His purposes.

4. Cast your cares on Jesus.

5. Humble yourself before Jesus.

6. Obey Jesus, even when it doesn't make sense.

7. Abide in Jesus.

You have the strength and power to do all things through Christ Jesus (Philippians 4:13). Pursue Him. Spend time with Him. Honor Him. Speak His name to others. Magnify Him. Then watch Him work on your behalf.

On Your Own

1. In *The Power of Jesus' Names*, Dr. Evans shares his favorite Scripture verse—Galatians 2:20. Read the verse and answer the following questions.

   a. What practical steps can you take to incorporate the meaning of this verse into your own life?

   b. Would you be willing to pray the content of this verse every morning before you get out of bed? If so, write a prayer in your own words based on this verse.

2. In this study we've looked at many character qualities and attributes of Jesus through some of His names—attributes such as…

compassion	humility
restraint	forthrightness
power over sin and opposition	commitment to God's kingdom
love	and rule

To make this very visual for you, use the circle below to create a pie chart. If each of these qualities of Jesus are present in your life, how big would say each "slice" is?

As you look at your completed chart, what do you think can be done to grow the character qualities that are currently the smallest "slices"?

3. As you conclude your time in this study, reflect on these words from Dr. Evans.

You have to give Christ permission to let His anointing flow through you. How do you do that? By faith in the Son of God. By tapping into His truth and applying His rule, forgiveness, standard, and Word over every part of your life. By boldly approaching the throne of grace, knowing that no sin is too large to keep you from the presence of God, because within you is the mediating power of the Great High Priest. He is both your ruler and the overruler of circumstances and challenges in your life.

Living by faith in the Son of God requires letting go of living by the flesh. You can no longer operate based on confidence in your own self, thoughts, and abilities. The way you access heaven's power and get it to fully operate in your life is through a complete reliance on and obedience to Christ. Be yoked with Christ (Matthew 11:29-30). It is He who must work for you. Yes, you have talents. Yes, you have discernment. Yes, you have effort. But none of that will amount to anything long lasting apart from the overarching rule, power, and involvement of Christ. It is He who is to speak through you as prophet. It is He who is to bring You mercy and confidence as you boldly enter the presence of the Father because He is the priest. It is He who will instruct you on what you are to do because He rules over you as King. To the degree that you rely on and remain in union with Christ is the same degree to which you will access His benefits and rewards in this life and the next.

Relying on Christ and resting in Christ for all things is the greatest life strategy you could ever apply. The closer you draw to Him and the more you allow His words to become your own, the more you will experience the fulfillment of the purpose for which you were placed here on earth.

The Power of Jesus' Names, pages 198-199

a. What are some intentional steps you can implement to help you rely on Jesus more fully and reflect Him more authentically in your life?

b. Take a moment to thank Jesus for this time of study on His names. Invite Him into an even more regular, intimate fellowship with you so that He can impact your thoughts, words, and actions more than He has ever done before.

Dr. Tony Evans and The Urban Alternative

About Dr. Tony Evans

Dr. Tony Evans is founder and senior pastor of the 10,000-member Oak Cliff Bible Fellowship in Dallas, founder and president of the Urban Alternative, chaplain of the NBA's Dallas Mavericks, and author of many books, including *Destiny* and *Victory in Spiritual Warfare*. His radio broadcast, *The Alternative with Dr. Tony Evans*, can be heard on more than 1,300 outlets and in more than 130 countries.

The Urban Alternative

The Urban Alternative (TUA) equips, empowers, and unites Christians to impact individuals, families, churches, and communities through a thoroughly kingdom agenda worldview. In teaching truth, we seek to transform lives.

The core cause of the problems we face in our personal lives, homes, churches, and societies is spiritual; therefore, the only way to address it is spiritually. We've tried a political, social, economic, and even a religious agenda. It's time for a kingdom agenda—the visible manifestation of the comprehensive rule of God over every area of life.

The unifying, central theme of the Bible is the glory of God and the advancement of His kingdom. This is the conjoining thread from Genesis to Revelation—from beginning to end. Without that theme, the Bible might look like disconnected stories that are inspiring but seem to be unrelated in purpose and direction. The Bible exists to share God's movement in history to establish and expand His kingdom. Understanding that increases the relevance of these ancient writings in our day-to-day living because the kingdom is not only then—it is now.

The absence of the kingdom's influence in our own lives and in our families, churches, and communities has led to a catastrophic deterioration in our world.

- People live segmented, compartmentalized lives because they lack God's kingdom worldview.

- Families disintegrate because they exist for their own satisfaction rather than for the kingdom.

- Churches have limited impact because they fail to comprehend that the goal of the church is not to advance the church itself, but the kingdom.

- Communities have nowhere to turn to find real solutions for real people who have real problems, because the church has become divided, ingrown, and powerless to transform the cultural landscape in any relevant way.

The kingdom agenda offers us a way to live with a solid hope by optimizing the solutions of heaven. When God and His rule are not the final and authoritative standard over all, order and hope are lost. But the reverse of that is true as well—as long as we have God, we have hope. If God is still in the picture, and as long as His agenda is still on the table, it's not over.

Even if relationships collapse, God will sustain you. Even if finances dwindle, God will keep you. Even if dreams die, God will revive you. As long as God and His rule guide your life, family, church, and community, there is always hope.

Our world needs the King's agenda. Our churches need the King's agenda. Our families need the King's agenda.

In many major cities, drivers can take a loop to get to the other side of the city without driving straight through downtown. This loop takes them close enough to the city to see its towering buildings and skyline, but not close enough to actually experience it.

This is precisely what our culture has done with God. We have put Him on the "loop" of our personal, family, church, and community lives. He's close enough to be at hand should we need Him in an emergency, but far enough away that He can't be the center of who we are.

Sadly, we often want God on the loop of our lives, but we don't always want the King of the Bible to come downtown into the very heart of our ways. Leaving God on the loop brings about dire consequences, as we have seen in our own lives and with others. But when we make God and His rule the centerpiece of all we think, do, and say, we experience Him in the way He longs for us to.

He wants us to be kingdom people with kingdom minds set on fulfilling His kingdom purposes. He wants us to pray as Jesus did—"Not My will, but Yours be done" (Luke 22:42)—because His is the kingdom, the power, and the glory.

There is only one God, and we are not Him. As King and Creator, God calls the shots. Only when we align ourselves underneath His comprehensive authority will we access His full power and authority in our lives, families, churches, and communities.

As we learn how to govern ourselves under God, we will transform the institutions of family, church, and society according to a biblically based, kingdom worldview. Under Him, we touch heaven and change earth.

To achieve our goal, we use a variety of strategies, approaches, and resources for reaching and equipping as many people as possible.

Broadcast Media

Millions of individuals experience *The Alternative with Dr. Tony Evans*, a daily broadcast playing on nearly 1,3000 radio outlets and in more than 130 countries. The broadcast can also be seen on several television networks, online at TonyEvans.org, and on the free Tony Evans app. More than four million message downloads occur each year.

Leadership Training

The *Tony Evans Training Center (TETC)* facilitates educational programming that embodies the ministry philosophy of Dr. Tony Evans as expressed through the kingdom agenda. The training courses focus on leadership development and discipleship in five tracks:

- Bible and theology
- personal growth
- family and relationships
- church health and leadership development
- society and community impact

Kingdom Agenda Pastors (KAP) provides a viable network for like-minded pastors who embrace the kingdom agenda philosophy. Pastors have the opportunity to go deeper with Dr. Tony Evans as they are given greater biblical knowledge, practical applications, and resources to impact individuals, families, churches, and communities. KAP welcomes senior and associate pastors of all churches. KAP also offers an annual summit, held each year in Dallas, Texas, with intensive seminars, workshops, and resources.

Pastors' Wives Ministry, founded by Dr. Lois Evans, provides counsel, encouragement, and spiritual resources for pastors' wives as they serve with their husbands in ministry. A primary focus of the ministry is the KAP Summit, which offers senior pastors' wives a safe place to reflect, renew, and relax along with training in personal development, spiritual growth, and care for their emotional and physical well-being.

Community Impact

National Church Adopt-a-School Initiative (NCAASI) empowers churches across the country to impact communities through public schools, effecting positive social change in urban youth and families. Leaders of churches, school districts, faith-based organizations, and other non-profit organizations are equipped with the knowledge and tools to forge partnerships and build strong social service delivery systems. This training is based on the comprehensive church-based community impact strategy conducted by Oak Cliff Bible Fellowship. It addresses areas such as economic development, education, housing, health revitalization, family renewal, and racial rec-onciliation. NCAASI assists churches in tailoring the model to meet specific needs of their com-munities, while addressing the spiritual and moral frame of reference. Training events are held annually in the Dallas area at Oak Cliff Bible Fellowship.

Athlete's Impact (AI) is an outreach into and through sports. Coaches are sometimes the most influential adults in young people's lives—even more than parents. With the rise of fatherlessness in our culture, more young people are looking to their coaches for guidance, character develop-ment, practical needs, and hope. Athletes (professional or amateur) also influence younger athletes and kids. Knowing this, we equip and train coaches and athletes to live out and utilize their God-given roles for the benefit of the kingdom. We aim to do this through our iCoach App, weCoach Football Conference, and other resources, such as *The Playbook: A Life Strategy Guide for Athletes*.

Resource Development

We foster lifelong learning partnerships with the people we serve by providing a variety of published materials. Dr. Evans has published more than 100 unique titles (booklets, books, and Bible studies) based on more than 40 years of preaching. Our goal is to strengthen individuals in their walk with God and service to others.

For more information and a complimentary copy of Dr. Evans' devotional newsletter,

call (800) 800-3222

or write
TUA
PO Box 4000
Dallas TX 75208

or visit www.tonyevans.org

YOUR *Eternity* IS OUR *Priority*

At The Urban Alternative, eternity is our priority—for the individual, the family, the church and the nation. The 45-year teaching ministry of Tony Evans has allowed us to reach a world in need with:

The Alternative – Our flagship radio program brings hope and comfort to an audience of millions on over 1,300 radio outlets across the country.

tonyevans.org – Our library of teaching resources provides solid Bible teaching through the inspirational books and sermons of Tony Evans.

Tony Evans Training Center – Experience the adventure of God's Word with our online classroom, providing at-your-own-pace courses for your PC or mobile device.

Tony Evans app – Packed with audio and video clips, devotionals, Scripture readings and dozens of other tools, the mobile app provides inspiration on-the-go.

Explore God's kingdom today.
Live for more than the moment.
Live for *eternity.*

tonyevans.org

Life is busy,
but Bible study is still possible.

*a **portable** seminary*

Explore the kingdom.
Anytime, anywhere.

*Subscription model

TONY EVANS
TRAINING CENTER

tonyevanstraining.org